Dorothy Millar.
was a M.M's

PLACES CHRIST HALLOWED
On Seeing the Holy Land

by

HERCHEL H. SHEETS

The Upper Room
The World's Most Widely Used Devotional Guide
and
Other Devotional Literature
1908 Grand Avenue
Nashville, Tennessee 37203

Library of Congress Catalog Card Number: 65-19532

The Scripture quotations in this volume are from the Revised Standard Version of the Holy Bible, copyrighted by the division of Christian Education of the National Council of Churches of Christ in the United States of America, and are used by permission.

PICTURE CREDITS: Pages 12, 24, 28, 36, and 56, Religious News Service Photo, New York, N. Y.; 8, 40, and 44, H. Armstrong Roberts, Philadelphia, Pa.; 48 and 52, from Three Lions; 3, George Pickow, from Three Lions, New York, N. Y.; 16 and 20, Israel Information Services, New York, N. Y.; and 32, Wide World Photos, New York, N. Y.

UR-208-15-0465
Printed in the United States of America

The Upper Room near Jerusalem

EDITOR'S PREFACE

Here is a small book in which the author has given us a perspective not only of the land of Jesus but also of the important events in His life and ministry two thousand years ago. One needs this perspective whether he is making a visit to the Holy Land or beginning a study of it or just casually reading about it.

Today thousands of tourists visit the Holy Land. Most of these are religious people who go because of their love for Christ. With this little book as a background, one can visit more intelligently and with more understanding. Whether one can visit the Holy Land or not, he longs to "walk where Jesus walked." This devotional book will help persons do that. Those who want to learn more about the important places in the life of Jesus and their biblical significance can benefit from it. The pictures will be helpful in making the places real.

This book should have a wide use. The chapters are arranged according to the chronology of the events in the life of Jesus and make for interesting and easy reading. The scripture passages given at the end of each chapter will be most valuable in relating the Bible information to the places. The book will be used by many in preparation for a trip to the Holy Land. Pastors will find it helpful in arranging group studies on the holy places. We hope the book will have wide acceptance and we recommend it for use in the churches. Mr. Joginder Sandhu has been the chief editor.

—J. Manning Potts

CONTENTS

INTRODUCTION

Things receive their value not simply on the basis of their inherent worth, but also on the basis of their associations. If someone in a high position, or someone we especially love or esteem, has possessed or touched an object, that gives it a value it would not otherwise have.

Marjorie Wilson, the author, actress, and lecturer, tells of sitting in a restaurant one day with a lady who was reading one of Dr. Frank Crane's articles in a newspaper. She was so enthusiastic about it that she read portions of it aloud. It so happened that Miss Wilson had been a guest in the Crane home the night before and was wearing a chrysanthemum he had given her. She could not resist telling her new friend about it, but she was not prepared for the response she made. She began staring at the chrysanthemum as though it had been dropped from heaven, and then she tried to buy it. She said, "I'll give you anything you ask for it. Just think, he had that in his house, he touched it!"

This is also true of places. Have you ever noticed how meaningless the name of a place is until one associates some person or event with it? That is why the study of geography takes on new interest when it is approached from an historical point of view. We are not very likely to be interested in a place unless we know something that has happened there or some person of some importance to us who has been associated with it.

The land of Palestine is in many ways a rather insignificant land. It is not large enough nor wealthy enough nor beautiful enough to command recognition. Yet to millions of people, it is "The Holy Land," because of events which took place there many centuries ago. It is an especially significant land to Christians because Jesus "touched it." The earthly life of our Lord was lived out on this relatively small and insignificant portion of the earth's surface. But how He hallowed the places He touched!

If those places could talk, they would have some marvelous messages for us. Well, they have them anyway. When we become acquainted with them, they speak to us of the attractive and compassionate Man who touched them long ago. They echo His words, proclaim His deeds, and lift up His personality and character. And we, like many before us, are drawn into His redeeming presence.

We shall be looking, then, in the following pages at some of the places Christ hallowed—not simply to discuss them, but to see the Christ whose presence long ago made them sacred. May His Person and message become more real to us as we do!

—Herchel H. Sheets
Canton, Georgia

Let us go over to Bethlehem.

I

The Town of His Birth

"Let us go over to Bethlehem and see this thing that has happened, which the Lord has made known to us." This was the word of the shepherds on the night of Jesus' birth. It is not likely that they had far to travel to reach Bethlehem. In fact, the traditional site of the Shepherds' Field is in clear view from Bethlehem. They simply walked across the hills to reach it. But since that night, multiplied millions have traveled across oceans and continents to reach it. So important did it become that night!

Bethlehem is located in the Judean mountains about five and a half miles south of Jerusalem. It is built on a gray limestone ridge at an altitude of about 2,500 feet. It is in the Jordonian section of Palestine, and is inhabited mainly by Christian Arabs.

The name "Bethlehem" means "House of Bread." That is an appropriate name, for it is situated in a rather fertile area. Today, as in biblical days, fine grain crops, figs, olives, pomegranates, and grapes can be seen growing around Bethlehem. The people are engaged primarily in agriculture and in carving mother-of-pearl and olive wood.

Bethlehem was never a large place in biblical days, but it had an importance far out of proportion to its size. It was the home of David, Israel's greatest and most beloved king. Here David had grown to young manhood as a herder of his father's flocks and had been anointed by Samuel as the future king of Israel.

David must have cherished many pleasant memories of Bethlehem. Once, while he was a fugitive from King Saul, he expressed a wish for a drink from the spring at Bethlehem. Three of his comrades heard him, and his wish was their command. They stole through the Philistine camp and brought the water to their beloved leader. But when David learned what they had done, he would not drink the water; he poured it out instead, for it looked as blood to him because they had risked their lives to get it for him. Thus he manifested one element of his greatness: The refusal to take lightly the cost to others of the good things which came to him.

Centuries after the time of David, at a time when Judah was experiencing some of her darkest days—the country had been defeated, cities had been destroyed, farms devastated, leaders exiled—some great soul spoke a word of hope to his people. He refused to believe the end had come for God's people. They would experience revival and triumph again, he said. And it would begin in a small place and in a small way: From Bethlehem would come forth One who would be the ruler in Israel and the instrument of God's redemption of His people.

After Jesus was born in Bethlehem, the New Testament writers remembered those words in the Book of Micah. A King indeed had been born in Bethlehem, and multitudes across the earth and across the centuries would bow before Him and pay Him the homage of their loving hearts.

Bethlehem is preeminently then the village of revelation. No wonder Christians are attracted to Bethlehem! God did something there He has never done anywhere else, though what He did there was to affect the whole world: He took upon Himself the garb of human flesh that He might make clear to men the kind of God He is, in order to draw them to Himself.

Since the time of Constantine in the fourth century A.D., there has been a church over the cave where tradition says Jesus was born. Constantine's church was destroyed in 521, and a new and larger one was built by Justinian I in A.D. 531. Further modifications were made by the Crusaders and others in the Middle Ages. Today the church is owned jointly by the Latin, Greek, and Armenian churches, each of which has a convent connected with the church.

The cave or the hollowed room itself is under the church. It is a rather gloomy place, lighted dimly by sixteen silver lamps and a shining star. Multitudes across the centuries have knelt here in this town whose name means "House of Bread" to give thanks for the birth of One who later spoke of Himself as "the bread of life."

RELEVANT SCRIPTURE PASSAGES:

The Book of Ruth
I Samuel 16:1-13
II Samuel 23:13-17
Micah 5:2-4
Matthew 2:1-23
Luke 2:1-20

He went and dwelt in a city called Nazareth.

II

The Town Jesus Put on the Map

The town of Nazareth is not mentioned in the Old Testament at all. It is mentioned in the New Testament twenty-nine times, but always in connection with Jesus. In fact, it would not be mentioned at all if it were not for Him. It is used simply as a means of identifying Him. "Jesus" was a common name in those days and so for purposes of identification the name of His hometown became a part of His name. He was called "Jesus of Nazareth." It was not that Nazareth was important, however; it was that Jesus was important. He gave Nazareth its significance. He put it on the map.

In the Annunciation sanctuary in Nazareth, which is built on the site where tradition says the angel announced to Mary the birth of Jesus, there is an altar on which are inscribed these words: "Here the word was made flesh."

Nazareth is situated in a basin in the hills of Lower Galilee, about seventy miles north of Jerusalem, twenty miles east of the Mediterranean, and fifteen miles southwest of the Sea of Galilee. The altitude is about 1,600 feet; the terrain is rough and rocky. A few miles south of Nazareth is the beautiful plain of Esdraelon; here was an international highway in Jesus' day. Jesus must often have looked out over that valley and recalled the momentous battles which had been fought there, and He must also have watched the caravans and Roman soldiers as they often passed by.

Another important highway was within view from a hill north of Nazareth. So, though Nazareth itself was an unsung village, a town with no name to nourish its pride, yet Jesus was not reared in the backwoods. Nazareth was near the world's thoroughfares. It was there—amidst the influences of a country village, but touched also by the influences of the wider world of the soldier, the trader, the traveler—that Jesus grew "in wisdom and in stature, and in favor with God and man."

When Jesus was just beginning His ministry, Philip felt the impact of His personality and went to tell Nathanael about Him. Philip had to identify Jesus by saying that He was from Nazareth, but his friend was not impressed; for he knew Nazareth, he lived near it, and he could not imagine anyone of importance coming from there. Nathanael had to see the person before he would credit the place with producing such a person. Nazareth no doubt contributed many things to Jesus' life, but it does not explain Him. He cannot be accounted for simply on the basis of geography and sociology. He was greater than His hometown, and so He gave it its place in history and the hearts of men.

Furthermore, He gave to all men everywhere an example and a challenge: No person needs to be imprisoned by his circumstances; through the power which God makes available, he can live in the world without being molded by it; he can associate with people without losing his individuality; and he can benefit from the good influences which surround his life without being ruined by the bad.

Nazareth today is inhabited mainly by Arabs, many

of whom are Christians. New Nazareth, growing up nearby, is populated mostly by Jews. Conditions in the city are somewhat backward, and one gets the impression that Christ has not made the difference there He would like to have made. But that was true during His earthly ministry also. When He went back to Nazareth soon after He began His ministry, He met with skepticism and rejection. His former neighbors and friends tried to push Him off a cliff to put an end to His "strange" talk! They had too little faith in Him for Him to do much good there. Perhaps they had been too close to Him to see His greatness, too familiar with Him to esteem and accept Him properly. But actually their tragedy was not that they knew Him too well, but that they knew Him hardly at all. Like many in our day, they could call Him by name and recite facts about Him, but the real person of Jesus was a stranger to them.

As one talks to officials in Nazareth today, he gets the impression that Nazareth still has growth ahead of it, and further history to make. But whatever else it may do, its real claim to fame is already established. Jesus put Nazareth on the map. It can say no better thing for itself today than that Jesus was from Nazareth. And Nazareth or any other town can do no better thing for itself than have Christ in its midst.

RELEVANT SCRIPTURE PASSAGES:
Matthew 2:23
Mark 6:1-6
Luke 2:39-41, 51-52; 4:16-30
John 1:43-46

Jesus came from Nazareth of Galilee and was baptized by John in the Jordan.

16

III

The River That Divided His Life

When one looks at the position of the Jordan River on a map of Palestine, he immediately realizes that it is a divider, for it comes down almost through the center of the country and divides it into two distinct parts. This made the river in biblical days an important landmark, and so most of the references to it in the Bible are of a geographical nature.

It is not the size of the river itself, however, that made it such a divisive factor. There are many rivers which are longer and wider and deeper than it is.

But it was the valley through which the river runs that made it the barrier and the divisive factor that it was. The Jordan Valley, which is from two to fourteen miles in width, is a part of the great rift valley, a valley with geological fault, which begins up in Lebanon and goes on down to Africa. Through most of Palestine the Jordan River is below sea level, and at the Dead Sea it reaches the lowest level on the earth.

Palestine itself is a part of the great rock of Arabia. But when the Israelites, after having escaped from the slavery of Egypt, crossed the Jordan and entered "the Promised Land," they were conscious of the separating influence of that river and valley. The tribes which stayed on the east side of the river felt it necessary to set up a special memorial to remind them that they were a part of God's people, too.

But the Jordan in this instance was not simply a geographical dividing line. Its crossing by the Israelites was an historical division also. They were never the same after that. A whole new life opened up for them, and they could talk now about "on this side Jordan" and "on the other side Jordan."

Jesus' life may be divided into two parts: Before Jordan and after Jordan. His baptism by John in the Jordan was the dividing line of His life. Never again would He know the ease and quiet He had known in Nazareth. From the Jordan He launched out into the world of men, challenging sin and evil, confronting and supplying human needs, and lifting men up toward God.

To some it has seemed strange that Jesus should step first into the Jordan before stepping into His career. He surely was not answering John's call to repent and return to God; He had never turned away from God. But He was identifying Himself with the "back to God" movement which John had started. He was taking His stand on the side of John the Baptist and was giving him the support of His person and His influence. Not to do so, He felt, would be to fail His heavenly Father.

He was not giving us instructions then about how to be baptized. He was calling us to identify ourselves with the causes that are dear to the heart of God—to get off the sidelines and into the arena of activity, to make our weight felt on the side of right. The emphasis is not on how we are baptized, but it is on whether or not we do so, and follow Jesus' way of life.

But He was doing more than this: He was also identifying Himself with the needy and sinful human race. Back in Nazareth He had felt keenly the joys and sufferings of His fellowmen. And as John called men to repent of their sins, this Man who had no sins of His own of which to repent went down into the Jordan, taking upon His own heart the burden of all men's sin—not that He might be a party to it, but that He might share its shame and redeem men from it.

No wonder Jesus received the assurance of God's approval of His life: "Thou art my beloved Son; with thee I am well pleased"! No wonder either that the Holy Spirit descended upon Him! He was receiving the equipment for His task. It was a gigantic task, and one which He could have avoided. But He would not stay away from the Jordan. He had come, He had acted, He had been empowered. It was "after Jordan" now in His life.

There ought to be a Jordan in our lives, too—a Jordan of decision, a time when we make up our minds about what we are going to do with our lives, about how we are going to invest them. This involves not simply the choice of a vocation, but, more important, the choice of values to cherish and goals to seek. The easy thing is to dream and to drift. The difficult, but wise, thing is to enter the Jordan of decision and come out ready to act. Then it will be "after Jordan" in our lives.

RELEVANT SCRIPTURE PASSAGES:

Joshua 3–4
II Kings 2:10-15
II Kings 5:1-19
Matthew 3:1-17
Mark 1:1-11
Luke 3:1-22

Ruins of the ancient synagogue at Capernaum on the shores of the Sea of Galilee, where Jesus healed the Roman centurion's servant

IV

The Town He Made His Home

Jesus grew up in Nazareth, but it is only in Capernaum that He is said to have been "at home." Capernaum was His adopted or chosen home. Quite early in His ministry, He went up above Nazareth to this thriving city on the northwest shore of the Sea of Galilee and made it His headquarters for His Galilean ministry.

That does not mean, of course, that He had a big and elaborate office. It means simply that He centered His Galilean ministry around Capernaum and that He spent a good deal of His time there. He may even have had a definite house in which to live. We know that several of His disciples were from Capernaum; so one of them might have opened his home to Him.

Capernaum is generally thought of simply as a small fishing village, but it was not as insignificant a place as one might think. The fact is that it was located near a strategic trade route from Damascus to Egypt and was a busy commercial city of about 50,000 people. The Romans considered it important enough to have a customs house and a military guard there.

The climate in Capernaum was quite warm, for the city, like the Lake on whose shore it was built, was more than 675 feet below sea level. The "geological spasm" which, centuries earlier, had formed the Jordan Valley with its river and three lakes, had left a good many hot sulphur springs in its wake. People came from far and near during biblical days to bathe in those springs, seeking healing from disease and relief from suffering. It is very likely that some who found healing at a word or touch from this new Teacher and Physician had already experienced disappointment in the failure of those springs to heal them.

Faith was required for Jesus' miracles of healing. He had found very little faith in Nazareth, but He must have found a lot in and around Capernaum, for we know He performed many miracles there. There was the faith, for instance, of the men who came bringing a paralytic friend for Jesus to heal. He was in a house, and they could not get to Him through the crowd. But their faith would not let them stop. They climbed up on the roof, removed a part of it, and let their friend down through the hole into the presence of Jesus. "And when Jesus saw their faith," a new day dawned for their friend!

One of the ways to discover a person's true character is to note the things which cause him to rejoice. Nothing gave Jesus greater joy than to see some person manifest real faith. We are told that the faith of one person in Capernaum caused Him to marvel. The person was a Roman centurion, a non-Jew. But his sympathies were with the Jews, for he had built them a synagogue. He wanted Jesus to heal his servant, but he felt unworthy to have Him come into his house. So he told Jesus just to speak the word, and he was sure his servant would be healed.

Today in Capernaum one may see the ruins of a third-century synagogue. It seems to have been built on the site of a first-century synagogue, perhaps the one this centurion had built for the people and the one in which Jesus taught. The Franciscans have memorialized this man by putting Jesus' words of commendation of him on a plaque on one of the stones of the old synagogue. Below Jesus' words they have written: "Capernaum calls us to boldness of faith, because the power of God and His readiness to perform miracles are far beyond the boldest desires of our believing."

But not everyone in Capernaum had that kind of faith. Today Capernaum is only a name in history and a one-mile strip of ruins. Jesus was not persecuted in Capernaum. The people tolerated Him; they even flocked after Him for awhile. But then, because they were disappointed in what He had to offer or because they were not willing to pay the price He demanded, they became indifferent toward Him.

Capernaum had an envious privilege. It saw Jesus' mighty deeds and heard His gracious words. But it shrugged its shoulders and said, "So what?" And the place He had chosen as His home and the scene of so much of His ministry became one of the places which disappointed Him the most.

RELEVANT SCRIPTURE PASSAGES:

Matthew 4:12-17
Matthew 8:5-17
Matthew 11:20-24
Mark 1:21-34
Mark 2:1-12
Luke 4:31-44
Luke 7:1-10
John 2:12
John 4:46-54

Sea of Galilee, the focal point of much of Jesus' ministry

V

The Sea in His Life

A visit to the Holy Land can be both inspiring and disillusioning. As one visits traditional sites of various places and events, he tends to grow skeptical about the authenticity of the sites—especially when two or more churches claim to be located on the correct site. He even gets to wishing that Christians did not feel it so necessary to memorialize every event in Jesus' life by building a church on the site of it.

So it is refreshing to come to the lovely Sea of Galilee. This is one place the appearance of which well-meaning Christians have not changed. No churches have been built on its waters and relatively few on its shores. Here one can be more sure than anywhere else in all Palestine that he is seeing the site as Jesus Himself saw it.

But though the Sea itself has not changed, the area around it has. Today the shores of the Sea of Galilee are rather sparsely populated, but in Jesus' day they were densely populated. There were at least nine cities around the Lake itself, each with a population of 15,000 or more; and at least one, Capernaum, had about 50,000.

The district of Galilee was the most northerly district in the country. It was about 50 miles long and 25 miles wide. Its focal point was this heart-shaped, fresh-water lake, about thirteen miles long and eight miles wide at its widest point. Here was the center of Galilean life. Most roads in the district passed to or near this lake, and travelers and merchants converged about it. The major occupations were fishing and fish-curing (salted fish were sent out from the lake in all directions), boat-building, agriculture and fruit-growing, and dyeing and tanning.

In the Old Testament period, this lake was called "Chennereth," because of a small, fertile plain by that name on its northwest shore. The plain was also called "Gennesaret," and so the lake, in the Gospels, is sometimes called "the lake of Gennesaret." In the later New Testament period, it was called the sea of Tiberias, after Herod Antipas's capital city which he built on the southwest shore of the lake about A.D. 25.

The Sea of Galilee is surrounded almost completely by mountains, and since it is about 686 feet below sea level, its climate is understandably quite warm. At several points narrow gorges break upon the lake, and cold currents passing from the Mediterranean in the west are sometimes sucked down in vortices of air, resulting in the sudden storms for which the lake is noted.

Jesus' disciples knew about those storms, and, rugged fishermen though some of them were, they had a healthy respect for the storms. They were even frightened by them at times. On one occasion, they became impatient with Jesus when they found Him sleeping soundly while they battled the storm. They were not only in a storm, but a storm was in them also— a storm of fear and doubt. At a word from Jesus, however, the storm subsided.

That happens again and again even today. When one becomes sure that Christ is on some tumultuous scene with him, his fears subside, and his faith surges forth anew!

The people of Galilee, being some distance from Jerusalem, had not been as strongly under the constraint of the religious leaders as had the Jews who lived farther south in Judea. Since there were more non-Jews in this area than in any other district in the country, they had been more exposed to pagan or non-Jewish ideas.

Jesus, of course, was a Galilean himself, and when He began His ministry, He left Nazareth and went to the focal point of the district and centered His ministry there. Several of the men He selected as disciples lived near the Sea of Galilee and made their living on it. It must have been a dear place to Him, too. He taught from boats on its waters, used it for travel, and sometimes sought rest and release from the crowds by crossing to its opposite shores.

The rabbis said, "Jehovah hath created seven seas, but the Sea of Gennesaret is his delight." Perhaps it is God's favorite. However, we know it is the favorite of the Christians, for it is the sea in the life of their Lord, the one He hallowed with His gracious presence.

RELEVANT SCRIPTURE PASSAGES:

Numbers 34:1-12
Matthew 4:18-25
Mark 3:7-12
Mark 4:35-41
Luke 5:1-11
John 6:1-21
John 21:1-14

The site of Jacob's well, where Jesus rested and asked a Samaritan woman for a drink of water

VI

The Well Beside Which He Rested

"Jesus, wearied as he was with his journey, sat down beside the well." The Gospel of John, which is so intent on showing us the divine Christ, gives us also this picture of the tired Christ. He must have felt this way many times, for He traveled a great deal, and most of His traveling was by foot.

On this particular day, He had been in the mountains and valleys of Samaria. This was the central part of the country, an area inhabited mainly by descendants of Hebrews who had intermarried with foreigners brought into the area by the Assyrian conquerors in the eighth century B.C. There had long been strife between these people, called Samaritans, and the Judeans or Jews. It dated back to the period of the return from the Exile in the sixth and fifth centuries B.C. when the Judeans had refused to allow the Samaritans to join them in rebuilding the Temple and the walls of Jerusalem. Thus rebuffed, in the fourth century B.C. the Samaritans had built a temple of their own on Mount Gerizim, but it had been destroyed in 129 B.C. by John Hyrcanus I, a Jewish king and high priest.

The well beside which Jesus rested that day was at the foot of Mount Gerizim, and it was toward this mountain that the Samaritan woman pointed when she said, "Our fathers worshiped on this mountain." The descendants of this woman still worship there. There are only a few hundred Samaritans left, and their headquarters is at Nablus, about a mile and a half north of

Jacob's well. They have a synagogue in Nablus, but they go to the top of the mountain to observe the feast of the Passover and some of their other festivals.

The Old Testament does not tell us of any well Jacob dug here, but we do know that he settled here for a time after his return from Mesopotamia. There are several streams in this area, but Jacob may have dug the well to lessen the possibility of conflict with the native residents of the area.

Today the traditional "Jacob's well" is in a walled enclosure, owned by the Greek Orthodox Church. As early as the fourth century A.D., a church was built on the site. The Crusaders built a new church on the same foundation, and now the Greek Orthodox are building one on the same spot (begun in 1914, but still unfinished). The well is reached by going down a stairway below ground into the remains of the crypt of the Crusaders' church.

A stone curb covers the top of the well. The well itself is between 75 and 100 feet deep; its diameter is about seven and one-half feet, except near the top where it is smaller. The upper part of the well, which was cut through soil and clay, has been lined with masonry, but the lower part was cut through soft limestone. It is both a cistern and a spring, for it is fed by surface water as well as by underground sources. Its water is cool and refreshing.

On that occasion when Jesus came there, this well was the scene of several surprises. The Samaritan woman who came to draw water from the well was surprised when the strange Jew she found there ignored custom and asked her for a drink of water. But that was only the beginning of her surprises. She was surprised most by His understanding of her, His power to look to the depths of her being and discern her true character. No one else had ever been able to read the contents of her heart so clearly and completely.

The disciples were surprised, too. They were surprised, on their return from the village where they had gone to buy food, to find their Teacher, contrary to strong custom, talking publicly with a woman, and that a Samaritan. They were surprised also that He was no longer hungry. They could not understand that to Him the experience of seeing a human soul awakened and started on its way to real life was more important than food and drink.

Jesus "rested" beside Jacob's well, and it is there today as a symbol of a concern that knows no prejudice and of a love which is like the cool water of a bubbling spring.

RELEVANT SCRIPTURE PASSAGES:

Genesis 33:18-20
John 4:1-42

A section of the ancient walls of Jericho in ruin, with recent buildings in the background

VII

The Town Where He Stopped

In 1894, George Adam Smith made this summary statement about Jericho: "No great man was born in Jericho; no heroic deed was ever done in her. She has been called 'the key' and 'the guardhouse' of Judea; she was only the pantry. She never stood a siege, and her inhabitants were always running away."

Geography throws some light on these statements. Jericho is about fifteen miles northeast of Jerusalem and about five miles west of the Jordan River. One goes "down" from Jerusalem to Jericho, for the difference in altitude is about 3,300 feet. Jericho is about 820 feet below sea level; so the climate is very warm— miserable in the summer, but ideal in the winter.

The town itself is located on a fertile plain in the Jordan Valley, but the area around it is dry and desolate. The average rainfall is about eight inches per year, but one of the largest springs in Palestine supplies plenty of water for both domestic use and irrigation. This probably explains why Jericho is one of the oldest inhabited places in the world. Archaeologists have unearthed remains of human habitation reaching back to before 5000 B.C.

Since it was the city guarding the eastern border of Judea, Jericho was the first city conquered by Joshua and the Hebrews when they began their invasion of the land about 1250 B.C. So little remains of the Jericho of that day that archaeology can throw very little light on the destruction of the city. Joshua pronounced a curse on anyone who rebuilt Jericho, but it was rebuilt and has continued as an inhabited city to this day.

The warm climate of Jericho probably had something to do with the lack of resistance Joshua and other invaders encountered there. The people have never been noted for their skill or bravery in warfare. But the town was used quite often as a supply town and as a rest stop for armies. It is still a popular winter resort today. Fine oranges, bananas, dates, and vegetables grow there.

Herod the Great built the Jericho we read of in the New Testament, and made it his winter capital. Excavations show that it was a fabulous place. One building was about two city blocks in length, and one had a stairway 150 feet long. There were pools, parks, sunken gardens, and the normal civic buildings of a Greco-Roman city.

Herod had been dead for more than a quarter of a century when Jesus came through Jericho on His way to Jerusalem and the crucifixion, but it was still a fabulous place. Yet Jesus seems to have had no intention of spending any time there. The gospel writers picture Him "entering" the city, or "passing through" it, or "leaving" it. But as He is doing so, He is confronted by human need and He stops. A blind man calls to Him, and He stops to cure his blindness. A tax collector climbs a sycamore tree to see Him, and He stops to call him down from the tree and to go home with him.

To those accompanying Jesus, perhaps Jericho was just a place to pass through in order to reach Jerusalem, but to Him it was something more than that. It was a place to stop and minister to men's needs. Every place was like that to Him. He was never in too big a hurry or in too big a crowd to sense human need and to stop and minister to it.

More than once, Jericho had been the scene of heartless destruction. The Israelites had killed everyone in the city when they conquered it. King Zedekiah had fled to Jericho when Jerusalem fell to the Babylonians in 587 B.C. He was overtaken there, his sons were killed as he watched, and then his own eyes were put out. When Herod the Great was dying in Jericho, he ordered that some of the most prominent men of the city be put to death so there would be mourning at his death.

But when Jesus stopped there, there was no destruction, but only rejoicing, for sight was restored and lives were transformed! "Oh, that He would stop where I live!" we sometimes say. He does, if a sense of need and a hospitable spirit are there!

RELEVANT SCRIPTURE PASSAGES:

Joshua 6:1-27
I Kings 16:34
II Kings 25:1-7
Matthew 20:29-34
Mark 10:46-52
Luke 18:35 through 19:10

The town of Bethany as it looks today. Here Jesus found a home and the companionship of Lazarus, Mary, and Martha.

VIII

The Suburb Where He Lodged

"Leaving them, he went out of the city to Bethany and lodged there."

Bethany was a suburb of Jerusalem. It was located about two miles east of the city on the eastern slope of the Mount of Olives. Jesus and His disciples spent the nights there when they were attending temple ceremonies in Jerusalem. It was a rather insignificant village; it is not even mentioned in the Old Testament. But the New Testament references to it throw valuable light on the personality and ministry of Jesus.

We tend to picture Jesus standing before great crowds, teaching the multitudes. These are the scenes which have stamped themselves upon our minds. But Bethany reminds us how significant a part of His ministry was carried on in small groups or in homes.

He had no home of His own after He began His ministry, but more than a few must have opened their homes to Him. At least two families in Bethany did: Simon the leper, and Lazarus and his sisters, Mary and Martha. And since He was always about His Father's business, His ministry continued while He was in people's homes. In fact, it is not unlikely that some of His most effective teaching was done in homes.

What an experience it must have been to entertain Jesus! It was so precious an experience to Mary that she wanted to be close to Him every moment, fearful lest she miss a word He uttered. Martha wanted to be there, too; yet she could not forget the practical duties of a hostess. He ate food in people's homes, but He must have left them food for thought for days and weeks to come!

It is really not difficult to understand why Jesus was attracted to Bethany. He was from a country town, accustomed to space and fresh air, and Bethany was such a place. But He must also have been attracted by the companionship He found there. Jesus needed human companionship; it meant a great deal to Him. Mark tells us that one of the reasons why He chose disciples was that they might "be with him." At times, we see Him alone, alone with God. But there are other times, like the occasions of the Transfiguration and the struggle in the Garden of Gethsemane, when He wanted some of His closest friends with Him.

The Gospel of John speaks in the warmest terms of Jesus' friendship with Lazarus and Mary and Martha. All men were the objects of His love, but some responded more completely than others to His love. Lazarus and his sisters were among this number. Most of the people whose lives Jesus touched are left nameless in the Gospels, but these at Bethany are identified. And so we are given a glimpse of what fellowship with His friends must have meant to Him.

After a tense day in Jerusalem, to go out to quiet Bethany to the warm hospitality of the home of His friends must have been like passing into another world. In those last bitter days of His ministry, Bethany stands like an oasis of understanding and love in a desert of intrigue and hate.

It is no wonder that Bethany should be the scene of Jesus' ascension. Luke says, "Then he led them out as far as Bethany, and lifting up his hands he blessed them. While he blessed them, he parted from them." How appropriate that in this suburb where He had lodged with dear friends He should make His last appearance to His disciples!

Bethany is still there today. Its Arab name, "el-'Aziriyeh," is derived from "Lazarus," the friend at whose tomb Jesus wept before raising him to new life. The important thing, however, is not that there be a twentieth-century successor to the suburb that furnished His hospitality long ago, but that we all make our hearts and homes places of welcome and warm friendship to the lonely Galilean!

RELEVANT SCRIPTURE PASSAGES:

Matthew 21:17
Matthew 26:6-13
Mark 11:11-14
Luke 10:38-42
Luke 24:50-53
John 11:1-44

The Mount of Olives and the Garden of Gethsemane

IX

The Mountain of His Agony and Triumph

"And when they had sung a hymn, they went out to the Mount of Olives." It was not far—just across the Kidron Valley, east of Jerusalem. Jesus had been there many times before, and now He would go there once more to await His betrayer and arresters.

The Mount of Olives is a part of the main range of mountains running north and south through central and southern Palestine. It has the shape of a ridge about two miles and a half in length, with three summits, each of which today has its own name. The most northern summit, the highest of the three, is called Mount Scopus. It is 2,963 feet above sea level.

The most southern summit, which is the lowest of the three, is called the Mount of Offence or Corruption, for it is believed that it was here that King Solomon built places of worship for his foreign wives, thus offending God and corrupting the religion of Israel.

The central summit is called the Mount of Olives, though technically the name applies to the entire ridge. This summit is located just opposite the Temple area, and, since it is higher than the mountain on which Jerusalem stands, from it one has a clear view of the city. Its name, of course, was derived from the extensive olive groves which once covered the entire ridge. There are still olive groves there, some trees being as much as eight or nine hundred years old, but they are only a fraction of what they must have been in Jesus' day. Because it overlooks Jerusalem, this ridge has always been the camping ground of invading armies; and it is quite likely that most of the olive groves which Jesus saw there were destroyed by the Romans when they besieged Jerusalem in A.D. 70.

The Mount of Olives is mentioned only twice by name in the Old Testament. In one of the references (II Samuel 15:30), we have the pathetic picture of the aged King David fleeing from his rebellious son, Absalom: "David went up the ascent of the Mount of Olives, weeping as he went, barefoot and with his head covered; and all the people who were with him covered their heads, and they went up, weeping as they went."

The other Old Testament reference is in the Book of Zechariah (14:4). When the "day of the Lord" comes, Zechariah says, the feet of the Lord will stand on the Mount of Olives, and the Mount "shall be split in two from east to west by a very wide valley." The literal interpretation of these words led to the belief that this would be the site of the final resurrection of the dead, which explains why the Mount of Olives became a coveted burial place.

The Mount of Olives figures very prominently in the last days of the ministry of Jesus. He began His triumphal entry into Jerusalem from the Mount. It was while looking at Jerusalem from the slopes of this mountain that He wept over the city. He no doubt withdrew from the city occasionally during the last hectic days, to rest and to teach His disciples in the quiet of those olive groves. It was to the Mount of Olives that He retired with His disciples after His last supper with them. It was in one particular grove, the Garden of Gethsemane, on the lower slope of this mountain, that He struggled in prayer as He awaited the betraying kiss of Judas and the arresting hands of the Temple guards. And, after His resurrection, He led His disciples over the Mount of Olives to Bethany, on the eastern slope, before He was parted from them.

No wonder Christians have been attracted to the Mount of Olives! It is too intimately associated with Jesus for them not to do so. The view from the Mount of Olives is magnificent, but more important than that are the thoughts it inspires. Because of its associations with Jesus, these are long, deep thoughts.

Our Lord experienced both agony and triumph on the Mount of Olives. His experiences there call us to the spiritual perception which says, "Hosanna to the Son of David!" and to the dedication which says, "Not what I will, but what thou wilt."

RELEVANT SCRIPTURE PASSAGES:

II Samuel 15:30
II Kings 23:13-14
Zechariah 14:1-5
Matthew 26:30-35
Luke 19:28-40
Luke 22:39-53

A view of the old Jerusalem, the city over which Jesus wept

X

The City over Which He Wept

"When he drew near and saw the city he wept over it." It was an ancient city over which He wept. According to archaeological evidence, Jerusalem had been an inhabited place at least since the latter part of the fourth millennium B.C. Abraham found people there when he came to Canaan in the early part of the second millennium B.C. It was a chief city of the Canaanites, and the Israelites were not able to gain possession of it when they made their invasion of the land in the thirteenth century B.C. That remained for David to do, about 1000 B.C.

The city was called Jebus then, but after David made it his capital, it was frequently referred to as David's city. It has had other names during its history —Moriah, Zion, Salem, Ariel, Aelia Capitolina—but Jerusalem is the one which has outlasted all the others.

David's choice of Jerusalem as his capital was a shrewd political move. There was friction between north and south, and Jerusalem was neutral territory. It was also strategically located—on the central ridge of the hill country, about thirty-three miles east of the Mediterranean and fourteen miles west of the northern end of the Dead Sea.

The association of Jersualem with David served, in later generations, to enhance its importance to the Jews; for they had great reverence for David. But, even more important, it later became the religious center of the country, the sacred Temple being located there.

The destruction of Jerusalem by the Babylonians in 587 B.C. was one of the darkest moments in the history of the Jews, but they rebuilt the city after the Exile and made it again their religious center. It remained politically important, too, though the Jews did not have complete political independence again until the middle of the second century B.C.

When Herod the Great came into power in 37 B.C., he set out on a building program which gave Jerusalem a splendor and magnificence it had not known since the days of Solomon. Jesus saw Jerusalem in all its splendor, but He also saw the inward condition of the city—its seething resentment of Roman rule, on one hand, and its careless and sometimes calculated compromise with Greek and Roman culture, on the other. He saw there an emphasis upon rite and ritual to the neglect of sincere devotion, compassion, and service. And so He wept over the city.

Well, its splendor was not to remain for long. In A.D. 70, during the great Jewish revolt, the Romans completely destroyed the city. Later a new city was built on the same site and called Aelia Capitolina, but Jews were forbidden to even set foot in it.

When Constantine became the first Christian emperor of Rome, he began to build churches in Jerusalem to commemorate events in the life of Jesus, thus making Jerusalem "The Holy City" for Christians as well as for Jews. The Moslems gained control of the city in the seventh century, and except for about a century in the Middle Ages, when the Crusaders were in control of the city, it remained under Mohammedan rulers until the British took over in 1917.

Today Jerusalem is a divided city. Its walled area (the walls, about two and one-half miles around, were built by the Turks in 1542) covers much of the old city and, therefore, most of the Jewish and Christian holy places. It is under the control of the Arabs and is in the State of Jordan. Most of the new part of Jerusalem, which is much larger than the old, is west of the old city and in the Jewish State of Israel. In few places in the world today is there such a wall of hatred as in "The Holy City."

Jesus would still weep over it today. But the chances are that He would weep over some other cities, too; for the city over which He wept that day, like many another, was inhabited by people who were good and people who were bad. And Jesus' tears over Jerusalem were simply a revelation of the eternal heartache of God, as He surveys the human tragedy of sin and its consequences.

RELEVANT SCRIPTURE PASSAGES:

Genesis 14:13-24
II Samuel 5:6-9
Jeremiah 39:1-10
Nehemiah 2:1-20
Nehemiah 12:1-43
Luke 9:51
Luke 13:31-35
Luke 19:41-44

The south side of the old Temple place in Jerusalem

XI

The Temple He Loved

The first words attributed to Jesus by the gospel writers—and His only recorded boyhood words—were spoken in the Temple in Jerusalem. They were spoken to His tired and worried parents who had been looking for Him for three days. He said, "Did you not know that I must be in my Father's house?"

The magnificent Temple structures which meant so much to Jesus have long since been destroyed. As one looks down upon the city of Jerusalem today from the Mount of Olives, his eye is caught immediately by the beautiful Dome of the Rock. This is a large octagonal mosque, faced on the outside with slabs of marble and multicolored mosaics, and encircled with exquisitely inscribed quotations from the Koran. Though it has undergone numerous changes through the centuries, this building has been a place of worship for Moslems since it was first completed in 691 B.C., except for about a century when the Crusaders used it as a church.

Aside from being a very beautiful building, the Dome of the Rock has the distinction of being built over the large rock (58 by 44 feet) where tradition says Abraham was about to offer his son, Isaac, as a sacrifice to God. Tradition also has it that here David, toward the close of his life, offered a special sacrifice to God. Here, too, Solomon built his magnificent Temple, around 960 B.C.

Solomon's Temple stood until 587 B.C. when it was destroyed by the Babylonians. For more than half a century then the Jews had no Temple, but after their return from the Exile, they set about building a new one, dedicating it about 515 B.C. This was called the Temple of Zerubbabel, after the name of the governor at the time of its completion and dedication.

About 20 B.C., Herod the Great, who was not a Jew but an Idumean, got the consent of the Jewish leaders to build a new Temple for them. He built it on the same site as the old one, using specially trained priests to do the work. There was no interruption of worship at all during the building. The Temple proper was completed within two years, but the outer courts and colonnades were still under construction during Jesus' ministry. In fact, they were not completed until about A.D. 64, six years before the entire place was leveled to the ground by the Romans.

The Temple was larger than Solomon's building, and it was surrounded by a large paved court, bounded by extensive colonnades. It was in this area that the people congregated, except at the worship hours when there were separate courts for the non-Jews, the women, and the priests. It was here that Jesus did much of His Temple teaching, and it was here that He was found by His parents as a lad of twelve when He said to them, "Did you not know that I must be in my Father's house?" Here, too, He expressed His wrath on those who were exploiting their fellowmen in the Temple commerce and were creating in the Court of the Gentiles an atmosphere which made worship all but impossible.

Jesus loved this place, not because of its beauty and splendor, but because it was His Father's house. Yet

His heart was broken because He knew men were not using it aright, and that, as a consequence, tragedy awaited not only the Temple, but the city and the whole nation as well. That, however, did not cause Him to stay away from the Temple. Instead, He had what Robert Frost might have called "a lover's quarrel" with the Temple; He Himself used it aright, and He did what He could to make it what God intended it to be.

The destruction of the Temple in A.D. 70 put an end forever to the Jewish sacrificial system, and the Temple area has never again belonged to the Jews. Even today they are shut off from one of their most holy sites, "The Wailing Wall." This is a section (52 yards long and 59 feet high) of the wall which enclosed the Temple area in Jesus' day. Here Jews came for centuries, especially on the eve of the anniversary of the destruction of the Temple, to mourn their loss.

Yet their loss dates back beyond A.D. 70, for before they lost the Temple itself, they lost the spirit which should have characterized their use of it. May we not do the same in our day!

RELEVANT SCRIPTURE PASSAGES:

I Chronicles 21:18 through 22:16
I Kings 5 through 8
II Kings 12:4-16; 22:1-20; 24:1-17; 25:8-17
Ezra 1:1-11; 2:68-70; 6:13-22
Haggai 1:2
Luke 2:22-52
Matthew 21:12-17; 24:1-2

Kidron Valley near Jerusalem

XII

The Valley He Crossed

When David was fleeing from Jerusalem during the revolt of his son Absalom, a relative of King Saul—a man by the name of Shimei—came out and began cursing him and throwing rocks at him. David refused to allow his men to harm him. But he later warned Solomon to keep an eye on him. So Solomon had him come to Jerusalem to live and warned him never to leave the city again. "For on the day you go forth, and cross the brook Kidron," he said, "know for certain that you shall die."

The brook Kidron is the eastern boundary of the city of Jerusalem. It separates the city from the Mount of Olives. The bed of the Kidron Valley today is from ten to fifty feet above its level in biblical days; yet it is a steep descent from the Jerusalem plateau to its depth. The valley is dry most of the year, though water runs freely in it during the rainy season. In the early days of the monarchy, the water from the spring Gihon flowed through it to reach a tunnel to the pool of Siloam.

This valley, though rather small, has some very fertile land in it. So it is not surprising that some of it was owned, in Old Testament days, by the Davidic kings. Fine orchards and gardens may still be seen there today.

On the eastern side of the valley is located the village Silwan. Among its houses and shanties may be seen numerous rock-cut tombs, some of which date back to preexilic days (before 587 B.C.). Absalom, the rebellious son of David, had a monument erected to himself in this valley. A tomb called "The Tomb of Absalom" is found there today, though archaeologists say it is probably several centuries later than the time of Absalom.

The Kidron Valley figures prominently in the struggle between the religion of the Hebrews and the foreign cults. More than once pagan elements made strong inroads into the life of the nation, establishing themselves even in the Jerusalem Temple itself. Then when a good king, like Asa or Hezekiah or Josiah, came along, there was a purging of these foreign cults. This involved usually, among other things, the cleansing of the Temple. And it was into the Kidron Valley that the pagan instruments of worship were thrown and burned.

Two momentous crossings of the Kidron Valley are recorded in the Scriptures. One was David's crossing at the time of Absalom's revolt. With what heaviness of heart he must have made that steep descent from Mt. Zion into the valley below! He was in danger of losing a kingdom, but he knew he had already lost a son!

Jesus crossed the Kidron Valley on the night of His arrest. He had eaten the Last Supper with His disciples, and now He went out of the city, across the Kidron Valley, to the Garden of Gethsemane on the Mount of Olives, there to struggle in prayer and to be arrested by the Temple guards.

This was Passover time, and it was the practice to kill lambs to be eaten in the feast at the Temple and to pour their blood on the altar as an offering to God.

The blood of those thousands of lambs flowed from the Temple down a trench into the Kidron Valley. What thoughts do you imagine filled Jesus' mind as He crossed that valley that night? Here for centuries had flowed the blood from sacrifices men had offered for their sins. But before another day had come and gone, a new kind of sacrifice would be made—not by a helpless lamb, but by the strong Son of God. And, grateful men across the centuries would give thanks for Jesus' sacrifice, which takes away the sin of the world.

The two crossings of the eastern boundary of the Holy City, the Kidron Valley, were made by two heavy-hearted men. One, rejected by his son, cried out, "O my son Absalom, O Absalom, my son, my son!" The other, rejected by the world, prayed, "My Father, if it be possible, let this cup pass from me; nevertheless, not as I will, but as thou wilt."

Kingship was involved in both crossings. David was soon to be established as king again, but not for long; death came and ended his temporal kingship. But multitudes through the centuries, to this day, have believed Jesus to be their divine King and have given Him their loyal obedience in day-to-day living.

RELEVANT SCRIPTURE PASSAGES:
II Samuel 15:19-23
II Samuel 16:5-14
I Kings 2:36-38
I Kings 15:9-15
II Kings 23:4-14
John 18:1-14

The empty tomb

XIII

The Sites of His Crucifixion and Resurrection

In few places, if any, in Palestine today can one literally "walk where Jesus walked," for the passing of the centuries has naturally affected the land level. In Jerusalem, for instance, there are two or three places, inside buildings, where one can see portions of street pavement from the Roman period, but they are far below the present street level.

Yet every Friday afternoon the Franciscan Fathers have a ceremony in which they "walk where Jesus walked" from the area of Pilate's palace to the sites of His crucifixion and resurrection. Sometimes several groups, including a large number of pilgrims, participate, each group carrying a large wooden cross and making fourteen stops on the way, to remember the experiences of Jesus when He passed that way. At each stop or "station of the cross," certain prayers are prayed and hymns are sung.

The ceremony is concluded inside the Church of the Holy Sepulchre. This is a very large building, built over the traditional sites of the crucifixion and resurrection of Jesus. The first buildings were constructed here by the Emperor Constantine in the first half of the fourth century. Tradition has it that his mother, Helena, was led to the true sites through a vision. Hadrian's Temple of Aphrodite was demolished at this time, and two churches were erected, one on Golgotha and the other over the tomb. The present church, which was built much later, covers both sites.

For many people, viewing the inside of the church is both disappointing and confusing, for the sites have been altered so much that they do not look at all as one has always pictured them. The rock around the sites has been cut down to make the floor level. The tomb itself, a small cave, is in the basement of the church, standing in the middle of a large room. It is lighted dimly by forty-eight lamps and is guarded by a monk.

The plan of the church is very complex, with its numerous altars and chapels. Everything is pinpointed: There is the Flagellation column where Jesus is said to have been scourged, the Stone of Unction where His body was prepared for burial, the Chapel of the Apparition where He appeared to Mary Magdalene after His resurrection, and many other commemorations.

The authenticity of these sites has often been questioned, and for more than a century some have believed that the crucifixion and resurrection took place just north of old Jerusalem, rather than inside it. We know that burials did not take place inside the walls of Jerusalem in Jesus' day, but archaeologists cannot say definitely just where the northern wall ran at that time. The evidence points, however, to the sites being within the Church of the Holy Sepulchre.

The sites outside the walls are called Gordon's Calvary (for General "Chinese" Gordon, an early contender for the site) and the Garden Tomb. It takes imagination to make out the form of a skull in the rocky hill which is claimed to be Golgotha, but the Garden Tomb fits well the usual picture of the place of Jesus' burial. And though it is not as well attested as the tomb inside the Church of the Holy Sepulchre, it is, for many, more conducive to true devotion than the latter.

Perhaps we will never know just where it was that Jesus was crucified and buried, though we know it was not far from either site. But more important than locating the sites is appreciating the events. What matters is that on Calvary, wherever it was, Jesus spoke "love's last word," giving up His life for us; in the tomb He was buried and rose again, becoming "the first fruits of those who have fallen asleep." Because of this, He is now the ground of our hope and the promise of our deliverance from sin and death. That's what really matters!

RELEVANT SCRIPTURE PASSAGES:

Matthew 27:32 through 28:15
Mark 15:21 through 16:8
Luke 23:26 through 24:12
John 19:17 through 20:18

PERSONAL PRAYERS, NOTES, AND COMMENTS

PERSONAL PRAYERS, NOTES, AND COMMENTS